*PHOTOS BY ANDRÁS HÁSZ*
*TEXT BY GYÖRGY SZABÓ*

*CORVINA*

# HUNGARY

Translated by Christina Molinari

Photos © András Hász
Text © György Szabó
Design by Judit Erdélyi

ISBN 963 13 2806 6

Third edition

Printed in Hungary, 1989
Kner Printing House, Békéscsaba
CO 2756-h-8993

What is Hungary? From all the notions that come to mind when we look at it from the point of view of geography, ethnography, statistics, or any of the other sciences —whether we consider it from a historical standpoint or from our own feelings and expectations—we must have a certain image of it. Some people who hear about it and would like to find out more have trouble locating it on a map of Europe (although we all know we can locate it in the middle somewhere). Others immediately get an image of it based on what they have read, on stories and rumours. A few others living in the vicinity or just inside the border are quite familiar with it—which is to say, they know as much about it as they possibly can. So if we were to place all of these opinions and bases on a scale and examine them together, we would find that the scale would go on indefinitely, and everything related to our values about Hungary —our experiences, cultural backgrounds, interests, knowledge—would completely depend on which level of the scale we happen to identify with.

This diversity is only natural, though. During its thousand-year history Hungary has become a symbol in its own right. We might be able to pinpoint its external features by looking at some of the facts—that it comprises 93 032 square kilometres and its inhabitants number some 10.5 million—but this would by no means tell us what its essential characteristics were, and the task of trying to decide what constitutes those characteristics would itself be problematic. Hungary's scenic areas lack the stunning features—the topographical extremes—that usually draw tourists: perhaps the only notable exception is the *puszta*, located in Hortobágy and Little Cumania National Park on the Hungarian Plain, where we can still visit horse-breeding ranches or see herds and flocks roaming the plains and—with some effort —might even witness a mirage.

The greater part of Hungary is a country with gentle hills, crossed by rivers and streams. Springs often possess curative powers. Roman legions stationed in these parts during the days of the empire had already learned to set great store by them, naming the capital of Lower Pannonia province after Aquincum—a name which evokes the richness of the many sources of water they found. We may still see ruins from Aquincum in Budapest's city limits or, travelling a little further to what is present-day Transdanubia—the crumbling stones which were used to pave the roads of the former province and went to make up the pavement of the Amber Road running north. The foundations of guardtowers which used to defend the great fallen empire are visible at the bridge abutment by Gellért Hill, named after the cannonized bishop who, after coming from Venice to do missionary work in the 11th century was stuffed in a barrel by the Magyars and cast off the very same hill. On the other side of the Danube —long ago covered with oaks and marshes all the way to the unpredictable Tisza River—Attila the Hun's troops once assembled near Csepel Island and prepared to take the Roman troops by crossing on inflated goatskin "lifeboats". For a brief time Transylvania was also one of the empire's possessions and subject to Roman authority. The old Hungarian chronicles (which—to glorify the Hungarian nation—listed the Huns along with their leader, Attila, as putative ancestors of the Hungarian people) record that this land was rich in game and fish. Since then all that is left of this wealth is the game, and so even today the country is a hunter's paradise; but the sturgeon that were once enormous and often reached length of 8 to 9 metres no longer make the journey here from the Black Sea. Our rivers and streams are struggling with the hazards of the modern industrialized world. An enormous effort must be made to protect the "Hungarian Sea"— better known as Lake Balaton, the largest lake in Central Europe. What is today a popular resort attracting hundreds of thousands of people is also the site of several extinct volcanoes on the north shore where the Romans discovered wonderful soil rich enough for grapegrowing—just like that in the Tokaj area where the "king of wines" is cultivated.

The country—so serene, with a kind of Mediterranean beauty as you move south to Pécs and vicinity and so fertile in the Danube and Tisza basin—was hospital to both agrarian and nomadic ways of life. Hungary was primarily an agricultural country after the Magyar Conquest in the 9th century, with agriculture continuing to constitute a major sector of the economy up to the present day. Even considered on a par with world statistics, the yields of certain crops have been outstanding. Anybody who really travels across the country will see signs of this everywhere. The sustained agricultural achievements provide a link with the

past in a time when things are always changing and when architectural landmarks are somewhat hard to find: not a single castle has survived in its original state, and there are very few old churches or manors left—and it is very difficult to trace the historical development of towns.

A series of wars over a period of many years has been responsible for the destruction of national landmarks, a product both of civil strife and invasion by foreign troops. King Stephen I fought hard battles about A.D. 1000 when pagans rebelled against the new feudal order; the king was crowned by Rome, allied with Christendom, and went on to found the Hungarian nation. War broke out again in the 13th century with the first Mongol invasion. In 1526, entire central Hungary fell into the Turks' hands for some 150 years. Minarets or octagonal-shaped bath-houses with cupolas stand as reminders of that occupation. Those Hungarian fortifications that were left standing were blown up when Austrian troops came in to liberate the country in order to forestall any retaliation by Hungarian insurgents opposed to the union with the Habsburgs. Over the years the drive for national independence took the form of many movements, with Prince Ferenc Rákóczi II at the forefront in the early 1700s, and Lajos Kossuth leading the great "War of Independence" in 1848–1849. Sándor Petőfi— probably the best-known of all Hungarian poets—gave his life in battle during the struggle. The catastrophic events of 1848 were followed by the Austro-Hungarian Compromise of 1867, but this proved to be short-lived; the Monarchy was swept away with the advent of the First World War. Disastrous foreign and domestic policy turned the entire country into a theatre of military operations in the Second World War—the horrible memories have not been erased from the memories of the people, nor have they been effaced from the cities: although all of the bridges have been rebuilt, the outsides of buildings in the capital still show marks from the many months of fighting. Reconstruction was begun under a new social system—in a people's democracy, which was first experimented with during a trial revolutionary period in 1919.

Visitors to Hungary are often astonished by how little is left from the past. It is precisely because of the nation's frequently turbulent history that they do not find streets lined with buildings which have been preserved over centuries in the original state. What fragments from the past do remain in the relatively modern, 200-year old setting help us to envision what life was like during the time of the Árpád kings, or how people lived during the splendid days of the Renaissance. And traditional elements have been taken into consideration wherever new building has been planned; they have been incorporated region-wide, from cities down to tiny villages. András Hász has cap-

tured precisely this mixture of old and new styles in his photos, which not only reflect a sensitive—and oftentimes contemplative—attitude toward his subject, but will surely inspire the same reactions in his viewer. Traditional and contemporary worlds merge in this photo album which—in the spirit of a poem—shows us what it was possible to discover in the first place, but which our own eyes might have missed. Those who travel here with the intention of seeing everything slowly will find this the most rewarding approach to touring Hungary. What they discover will not be limited to technological advances—not confined to a certain level of material value—but will be filled with subtle beauty and even with a certain romance. Take a walk in the country where you can see for miles across the plain. Discover a grove on a hillside where folktales may have been spun, or a hamlet in a border town where the houses were built in a style reminiscent of Middle Age dwellings. Visit

a quaint old church which may have once served as a fortress, playing a double role of sheltering the dead along with the living, since they were frequently surrounded by cemeteries. Take a turn down an out-of-the-way cobblestone street, where turn of the century houses still exhibit eclectic designs unique to the Hungarian Art Nouveau. Or simply go to the top of one of the hills overlooking Budapest and see the view—with lights going on for miles at night, like tiny points of magic fire. We are the richer for these kind of impressions which will influence our thinking for years to come.

Visitors who come to Hungary are charmed by the country's old-fashioned hospitality. The warmth the Hungarian people show to newcomers is perhaps partly due to a national awareness that the Hungarian language isolates them from others. Languages related to Hungarian are spoken only by the Finns and several ethnic groups living to the north. Anyone

who visits Hungary will appreciate the great ease with which he can gain insight into the lives of the people. Lasting bonds may be formed anywhere in Hungary—whether they be with the land, the towns, or the people.

We can discover more of the country ourselves by this approach to travelling, where chance encounter will delight us and reveal singular beauty. True, each of us will take away a lasting and uniquely individual impression of Hungary. But our collective impressions—like a book filled with pictures—will become the common denominator, since what we have attempted to gain knowledge about radiates a character of its own to unify the diversity. This essential character is everywhere—we have encountered it during our discovery, and unravelled it cautiously but persistently, as though penetrating a human personality. Perhaps this is the reason that Gyula Illyés—one of Hungary's contemporary poets—considered acquiring knowledge synonymous with the

notion of Europe. Our knowledge, of course, will never fully coincide with absolute truth. But we have learned from the ancient Greeks that every approach to knowledge motivated by friendly curiousity will advance in the direction of understanding. May this album with its superb assortment of photos serve as a guide to learning more about Hungary. Whether or not the pictures coincide with our own experiences is something that all of us—already well-versed in the lore, excitement, and beauty of this land —will have to decide for ourselves.

*György Szabó*

**1.** Budapest: view from Gellért Hill

**2.** Here on the Danube's left bank—the low-lying, Pest side of the capital—is the neo-Gothic Parliament building, designed by Imre Steindl and officially opened in 1902.

**3.** Another look at the Parliament, here flanked by two bridges on the Danube: in the foreground is the Chain Bridge, the first permanent bridge in Budapest to span the wide river. It was planned by the English designer William Tierney Clark and constructed under the direction of his Scottish namesake, Adam Clark between 1839 and 1849 at the initiative of István Széchenyi, the great Hungarian reformer. The Margaret Bridge—built with the assistance of the French Eiffel firm—is in the background.

**4–5.** Vörösmarty tér—named after one of the most prominent 19th century poets—is the site of Gerbeaud's famous pastry shop and one of the main spots in central Budapest

**6.** The Paris Arcade (Párizsi udvar) passageways that lead to the shopping district in the centre of the city are crowned by stained glass arches

**7.** New hotels overlooking the Danube lend modern character to the old Pest promenade. The Forum Hotel

**8.** Kígyó utca attracts shoppers and browsers alike, sporting shop windows like the fashionable ones on other nearby lanes

**9–11.** Famous Váci utca, the crowded shopping district with busy stores and Haris köz

**12–13.** The city's representative avenue—Népköztársaság út—was built to commemorate the 1896 "celebration of the millennium", the anniversary of Hungary's thousandth year of existence; the first underground railway built anywhere on the continent runs below Hősök tere (Heroes' Square)—at the very end of the street—is the site of the Memorial to Hungarian Heroes with statues of outstanding figures from Hungarian history.

**14.** This unusual building stands further down from the square in the Városliget (City Park). Vajdahunyad Castle is an amalgam of dominant architectural styles through the ages in Hungary.

**15.** One of the popular recreation areas in the Buda hills near Normafa

**16.** Margaret Island is one of the capital's loveliest spots. It was renamed for the daughter of King Béla IV; St. Margaret once lived in a Dominican convent on the island.

**17.** Buda Castle—site of countless historical relics—rises above the city on the Danube's right bank. The Church of Our Lady—otherwise known as Matthias Church—may also be found here in the Castle District. The church walls with King Matthias' coat of arms bearing the date 1470 have undergone frequent reconstruction since their erection in the 13th century.

Almost all of the houses in the Castle District are from the Middle Ages. People simply come here to walk along the lovely streets.

**18.** Táncsics Mihály utca
**19.** Bécsi kapu tér
**20.** Országház utca
**21.** Fisherman's Bastion—one of the most distinctive areas of the city—is not part of the one-time Fortress, but a monument to Romantic architecture in the 19th century
**22.** Fortuna utca
**23.** The façade of Pest–Buda Restaurant
**24.** In front of Matthias Church

**25–27.** Budapest was established in 1873 when three independent cities united: Buda, Pest and Óbuda. Óbuda is the northern part of Buda, actually built on Aquincum, the one-time capital of Lower Pannonia province. The squares and little streets you see here have been reconstructed giving the neighbourhood a turn-of-the-century atmosphere.

**28.** The Danube Bend is just north of Budapest where the course of the Danube makes a sudden turn from east to south. The area is rich in natural splendour and historical treasures.

*Szentendre*—the first city on the road to the Danube Bend—is practically a part of the capital. Many Serbs have lived here since the 15th century, building their homes close together in charming, random fashion on a hillside by the Danube. Szentendre's beautiful location naturally makes it one of the most famous artist colonies in Hungary. Works by local artist are exhibited in numerous galleries throughout the city. Szentendre's attractions and proximity to the capital draw crowds of tourists year-round.

**29.** Rooftops in Szentendre
**30.** One of the local little restaurants
**31.** Courtyard with inner circle of boutiques
**32.** The Doll Shop
**33.** Houses in Szentendre
**34.** A crucifix in the main square
**35.** Main Square

*Visegrád*, a beautiful town in the Danube-bend was once a centre of royal power.

**36.** Researchers continue to excavate the remains from King Matthias' wonderful Renaissance castle

**37.** Castle fortifications consist of keep and citadel

**38.** A view of Visegrád Castle from the Danube

*Esztergom* is one of the highlights in this part of the country. Likewise a royal centre of power, for centuries the Hungarian see of the Roman Catholic Church has been administered here. The oldest relics in the city date back to the time of the Árpáds, Hungary's first royal dynasty.

**39–40**. The enormous cathedral built on the side of Castle Hill

**41**. The Castle chapel (built about A.D. 1200)

**42.** *Tata* is one of the scenic spots in Transdanubia with a 15th century castle which served as part of the strategic line of defence against the Turks.
The city of *Győr* lies at the concourse of three rivers, in the northernmost part of what was once Pannonia.
**43.** The new theatre in Győr
**44.** The fortress wall and Rába River
**45.** Köztársaság tér with Baroque buildings

*Pannonhalma*, the oldest Hungarian abbey, was built at the turn on the millennium on the top of a hill named after Saint Martin, who was born in the vicinty. The crown once worn by King Stephen, founder of the nation, was brought from the Pope by Asztrik, the Benedictine abbot installed in the abbey.
**46.** Church dating back to the 13th century
**47.** The famous library in the abbey
**48.** Cloisters in the monastery

*Fertőd* Castle—the most beautiful castle in Hungary and a masterpiece of Baroque architecture—once served as estate to the Esterházy family which played a major role in Hungarian history. The castle was one of the centres of Hungarian aristocratic life. Joseph Haydn lived here for a quarter of a century as conductor to the orchestra of the Prince. Music continues to play an important role in Fertőd where many concerts are still being given in the castle courtyard and state-hall.

**49.** A fountain in the park
**50.** Main façade of the castle
**51.** The state-hall

*Sopron* is one of the major cities in Western Hungary and one of the largest inhabited areas to escape the ravages of war. The places of historical interest there and lively cultural life attract many tourists.

**52.** Templom utca and the Fire-watch-Tower

**53.** Main façade of the Esterházy Palace (Templom utca 2.)

**54.** Façade of the house at Új utca 16.

**55.** Inside the courtyard (Templom utca 6.)

*Szombathely* was also built by the Romans (they called it Savaria) and was one of the stops on the famous Amber Road running north. Open-air performances given by the ruins of Isis Church evoke the festival-atmosphere of the old days.

**56.** The Garden of Ruins: remains of a former Roman road

**57.** Renaissance houses on Jurisics tér

*Kőszeg* is one of the most beautiful towns in western Hungary. The city made its outstanding contribution to Hungarian history when the tiny castle garrison led by Miklós Jurisics briefly staved off Turkish forces bound for Vienna during the siege of 1532. Narrow streets lined by old two-storey houses may be found in the centre of town which was once surrounded by a wall.

**58–59.** City Hall
**60.** The town's main square

**61–64.** The church of Ják—which once served as a Benedictine abbey—is one of the most beautiful Romanesque buildings in Hungary. Built at the beginning of the 13th century, the decoration on the chancel and main gate is especially ornate.

**65.** Őrség is located on the western defensive borders, where some enchanting styles in folk architecture have been preserved. Pityerszer, houses with thatched roofs.

The shallow and placid waters of *Lake Balaton*—the largest lake in Central Europe—attract many vacationers. The northern shore and surrounding highlands, where little communities line the sugar-loaf mountains are endowed with natural beauty. The mountains are primarily of volcanic origin. Little churches from the Middle Ages, "peasant-baroque" houses, and press-houses are also a distinctive part of the area.

**66.** Mary Magdalen Church at *Hévíz-Egregy*
**67.** The Calvinist Church of *Vörösberény* and surrounding wall which once served military defensive purposes
**68.** *Öskü*, Holy Cross Church
**69.** *Hegymagos,* press-house

*Tihany* peninsula on Lake Balaton has been inhabited since the Early Iron Age according to evidence provided by earthwork constructed on the peninsula. The stone cellars housed monks in the Middle Ages.

**70.** The abbey was built on the highest point of the peninsula and contains a deed of foundation which dates back to 1055. It was founded by King Andrew I, who is buried in the church crypt.
**71.** The organ in the abbey church, carved in Baroque style
**72.** The abbey overlooking Lake Balaton on Tihany peninsula
**73.** View of Lake Balaton from the Badacsony vineyards, also the site of grape-growing since ancient times ▶

Visitors who come to Lake Balaton remember the lovely scenery and enjoyable experiences their whole life long. Swimmers and sun-lovers join lovers of water recreation sports in coming back every year. Fishermen and worshippers of solitude can enjoy many peaceful hours relaxing on the reedy coast.

74. A beach in *Siófok,* the capital city on the southern shore
75. Enjoying the water
76. Neptun Hotel in *Balatonföldvár*
77. Fishing in the reeds
78. Sailboat
79. The "golden bridge"—sunset on Lake Balaton

Part of North Balaton once served as a formidable line of defence against the Turks, and *Nagyvázsony Castle* was a stronghold on that line. Every summer the castle hosts jousting tournaments which are historically authentic down to the costumes. These matches are dedicated to Pál Kinizsi who was a general in King Matthias' army. Kinizsi—who was a lord of the castle—was renowned for his courage and great physical prowess.

**80.** Paulite Church in Nagyvázsony with monastery ruins (dating back to about 1490)
**81.** Castle keep (15th century)

**82.** Statue of the Holy Trinity in front of the Bishop's mansion in *Veszprém*
**83.** Veszprém Castle (1765–76) was built on a great cliff in the Bakony Mountains north of Balaton. The Castle served as the Queen's residence.

A great many Roman relics have also been preserved in central Transdanubia. The area now known as *Tác* was once the site of the Roman *Gorsium*.
**84.** Roman tombs

In *Székesfehérvár* past and present styles exist side-by-side. Today a flourishing industrial area, it has actually been inhabited since the Romans and in the Middle Ages, and was the place where the first

Hungarian kings were crowned and interred.
**85.** Ruins from a medieval basilica in the Garden of Ruins
**86–87.** The Black Eagle, an old-fashioned apothecary in the heart of town
**88.** Bishop's mansion

Rolling country in South Transdanubia has a warm Mediterranean climate

**89.** The small church in *Mecseknádasd*, nestled in the Mecsek mountain-range

Transdanubia's capital city, *Pécs*, is one of the loveliest cities in Hungary with a warm southern climate and charming environs. The city is also an important centre in cultural life. Occupied since the Romans when it was known as Sopianae, many of its old buildings survived the turmoil it suffered over the centuries. ▶

**90.** Detail of an ornamental fountain which was sculpted at the city's famous Zsolnay ceramic workshop
**91.** The djami of Pasha Gazi Kasim on the main square; today it serves as the Central Parish Church.
**92.** The djami of Pasha Yakovali Hassan
**93.** St. Peter's Cathedral, a four-towered church dating back to the Middle Ages

*Mohács* is located on the lower reaches of the Danube. A famous battle was fought nearby in 1526, when Turkish forces wiped out Hungarian troops—a defeat which inaugurated the one-and-a-half centuries of Turkish domination. Mohács is also the site of an old folk pageant known as *busójárás* (Mardi Gras Procession). At carnival time when winter ends horrible masked figures parade along the streets.
**94–95.** *Busó* masks from Mohács

*Szeged* is on the banks of the Tisza, Hungary's second largest river, and it is an important centre in trade and cultural life in the south part of the Hungarian Plain. The flood which destroyed it in the 19th century took with it much of the city's past. Szeged is famous for its Open-Air Theatre-Festival each summer on Dóm tér.
**96.** Scene from a performance during the Festival

*Hortobágy and Kiskunság*—the famous Hungarian *puszta*—have been declared a national park to conserve the fabled beauty of one of Europe's most astonishing scenic areas.
◀ **97.** The famous Nine-arched Bridge in Hortobágy, the site of annual fairs
**98–101.** Scenes from the Hungarian *puszta*

*Kecskemét*—an important city for fruit-growing and processing and the place where famous "whistling" apricot brandy is distilled—is in the part of the Hungarian Plain. In the last ten years it has become an important centre in cultural life with the opening of the Kodály Institute, one of several internationally known workshops for instructing music students in the "Kodály Method".

**102.** The Cifra Palace is decorated with Art Nouveau motifs; the building in the background once served as a synagogue.
**103.** The façade of the Cifra Palace

*Debrecen*—"capital" of the Hungarian Plain—has the charm of an old country town. It was a centre of church reform during the Hungarian Reformation, the Calvinist College and the Great Church providing the backdrop for many significant events in Hungarian history.

**104.** The Calvinist Great Church
**105.** Inside the church

Many old wooden churches were built in northeast Hungary near the great forests. Painting and carving on sacramental objects and structures testify to the lively imagination of the villagers.

106. Panelled and painted wooden ceiling in *Tákos'* Calvinist Church
107. The church's pews were painted and inscribed

**108.** Detail: wooden belfry on *Nyírbátor* Calvinist Church (*c.* 1600)
**109.** Portal at the *Csaroda* Calvinist Church
**110.** Church choir

**111.** The gentle mountains overlooking the Tisza in the same part of northeastern Hungary, where world-famous *Tokaj* wine is fermented.
**112.** The *Füzér* Castle ruins in the quiet mountain landscape
**113.** Bodrog River

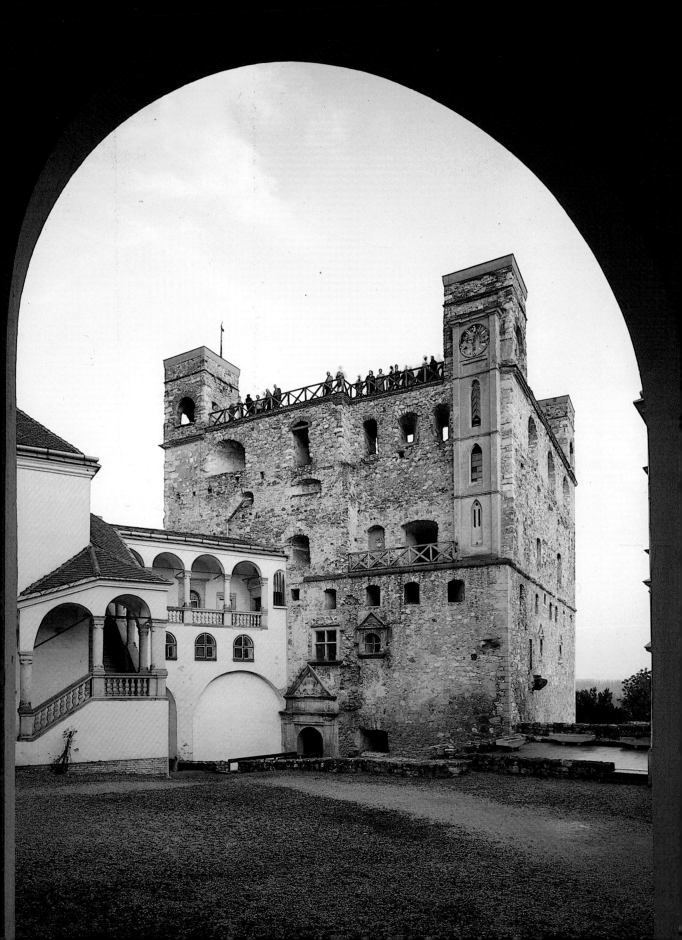

**114.** One of the most beautiful, well-preserved Renaissance castles is in *Sárospatak;* it once belonged to Prince Ferenc Rákóczi II

The city of *Eger* played an important role in the defence against the Turks. Excellent wines produced locally are kept in the network of cellars running beneath the city.

**115.** Looking out at the city of Eger
**116.** The village of *Hollókő*—one of the loveliest spots in the Cserhát mountains to the north—preserved the half-timbered houses and the 18th-century church

**117.** Ruins from a 13th-century Romanesque church in *Zsámbék;* it is one of the oldest in Hungary.